A TORAH IS WRITTEN

by PAUL COWAN

photographs by RACHEL COWAN

The Jewish Publication Society

Philadelphia · New York · Jerusalem   5747 · 1986

To Rabbi Joseph Singer

Copyright © 1986 by Paul and Rachel Cowan
First edition   All rights reserved
Manufactured in the United States of America
Library of Congress Cataloging in Publication Data

Cowan, Paul.
    A Torah is written.

    Summary: Describes the training, the materials, and the tools of Jewish scribes and the process
used to transcribe handwritten Torah scrolls.
    1. Scribes, Jewish—Handbooks, manuals, etc.—Juvenile literature. 2. Torah scrolls—Juve-
nile literature. [1. Torah scrolls. 2. Scribes, Jewish—Handbooks, manuals, etc.] I. Cowan,
Rachel, ill. II. Title.
BM659.S3C67   1986   296.6'1   86–10532
ISBN 0–8276–0270–7

Designed by Adrianne Onderdonk Dudden

This is a *sefer Torah*—a handwritten scroll that contains the laws and history of the Jewish people.

Wherever Jews have gone, the Torah has kept the people alive. Torah study has always been vital to Jewish life. In Israel, and in the Diaspora, *sifrei Torah*—the handwritten scrolls—have been read in synagogues every Monday and Thursday morning and during Sabbath and holiday services. These holy scrolls have transmitted Judaism from one generation to the next. The Torah is, in effect, the constitution of the Jewish people.

In many synagogues, before and after each reading, the Torah is carried to the congregation as part of a procession. Many people touch the covered scroll with a finger, a prayer book, or the fringe of a prayer shawl as a way of honoring it—and receiving honor themselves.

In every age, there have been *sifrei Torah* in virtually every community where Jews have lived. Each of these scrolls has been handwritten by a *sofer*—a scribe.

According to Jewish tradition, scribes perform one of the holiest of religious deeds: writing the words of the Almighty for the Jewish people. According to Jewish law, scribes must labor for the love of the Lord, not for wealth.

Rabbi Yehuda Clapman, an American-born scribe, lives in Brooklyn with his family. He has wanted to be a *sofer* ever since he was five years old. He still remembers the awe he felt in synagogue when he accompanied his father to the *bimah*—the altar from which the *sefer Torah* is read. While his father said the blessings, Yehuda used to marvel as he gazed at the columns and letters on the scroll in front of him. "It amazed me that they were handmade. I wanted to be a *sofer* from then on," he says. But at first he couldn't find a teacher.

When Yehuda Clapman was seventeen years old, Rabbi Eliezer Zirkind moved into his Brooklyn neighborhood. "I told him I wanted to be a *sofer*," Rabbi Clapman recalls. "He asked, 'Why aren't you?' I told him that no one would teach me."

"'I'll teach you,' Rabbi Zirkind said. He gave me all the ink, the parchment, the feathers I needed. He showed me what to do with the materials. I spent every available moment in his home. He never minded my looking over his shoulder while he worked."

Now, Rabbi Clapman is a fully trained scribe. He is eager to share what he knows. By teaching, he believes, he strengthens the future of Judaism. "The knowledge of everything that is Jewish belongs to every Jew," he says.

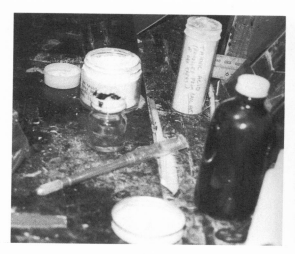 

Rabbi Clapman works near the window in the front room of his Brooklyn house. He is able to spend a great deal of time with his four children. He welcomes that opportunity. "They see me and they know what I am doing," he says. "I hope that fills them with a special feeling for the Torah."

When you watch the making of a *sefer Torah*, you are reminded that animals and minerals can have a holy purpose. A *sofer* uses them to create his most important tools—his parchment, his ink, and his quill.

But tools alone aren't enough. "When I was first getting started, I thought the parchment was the most important thing," Rabbi Clapman says. "Then I thought good ink solves every problem. Then I thought it was all in the quill. Now I've come to the true conclusion. You need all three to be perfect, and on top of that you need Divine help."

To make the parchment, Rabbi Clapman takes the skin of an animal the Torah defines as kosher—usually the skin of a cow—and soaks it in limewater for nine days. When it is a hairless surface, he stretches it on a drying frame. He scrapes the skin until it is dry. Then he sands it until it becomes a flat, smooth sheet on which he can write.

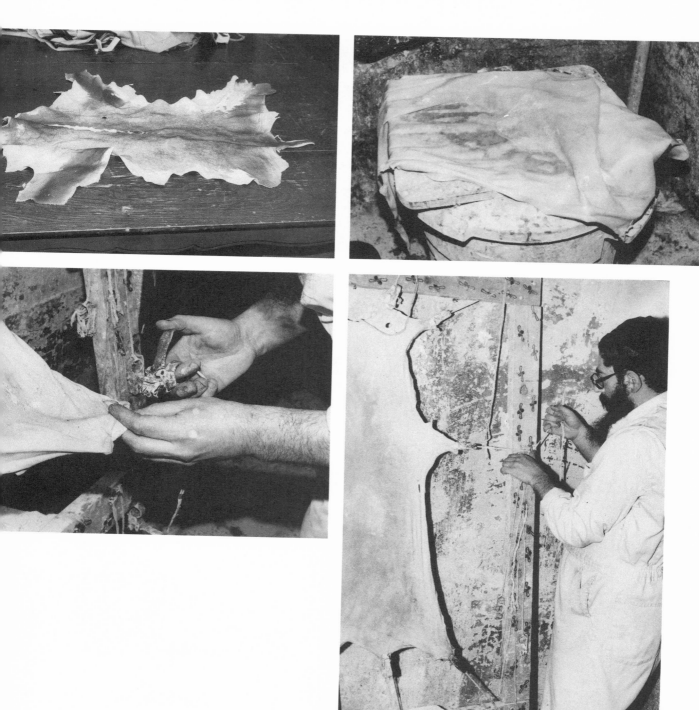

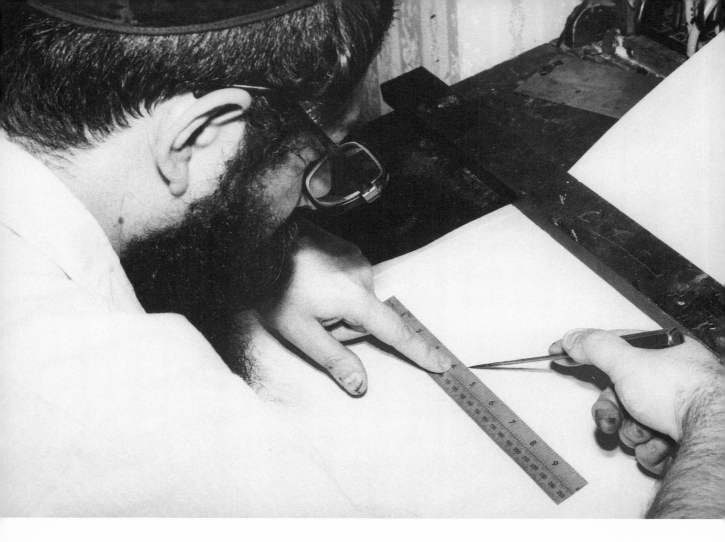

He then takes a straight edge and draws forty-three horizontal lines across the parchment, conforming to an age-old tradition. Then he draws two vertical lines to establish the boundaries for each column.

There are at least three columns to a sheet. They are three times as wide as the longest word found in the Torah—which normally means they are five inches wide.

As Rabbi Clapman prepares the parchment, he is careful to leave a blank margin of about four inches on the bottom, three inches on the top, and two inches between the columns, as required by law. That way, the creamy white of the scroll makes the flowing black letters seem especially vivid.

Now that Rabbi Clapman has made the parchment, he must make the ink. He blends gall nuts, copper sulfate crystals, gum arabic, and water; he wants the ink to be strikingly black. To be sure the ink is fresh, he makes only two teaspoonfuls at a time.

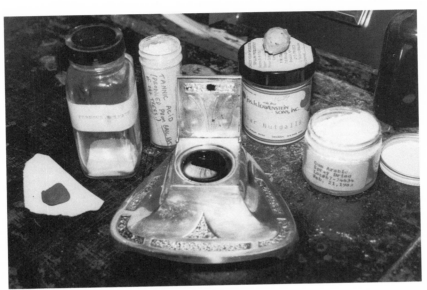

Without quills, the ink is useless. The shape of the quill is very important.

Most quills are made from the outermost five feathers of a kosher bird, such as a goose or a turkey.

Rabbi Clapman likes to use goose feathers because of tradition and because they are large and soft enough to help him write flowing letters. He always buys a large supply of them around Ḥanukkah, the only season of the year they can be acquired in New York.

A scribe writes with the stem of the quill, not the barbs. As a final preparation Rabbi Clapman uses a double-edged razor or a scalpel to put a fine point on the pen.

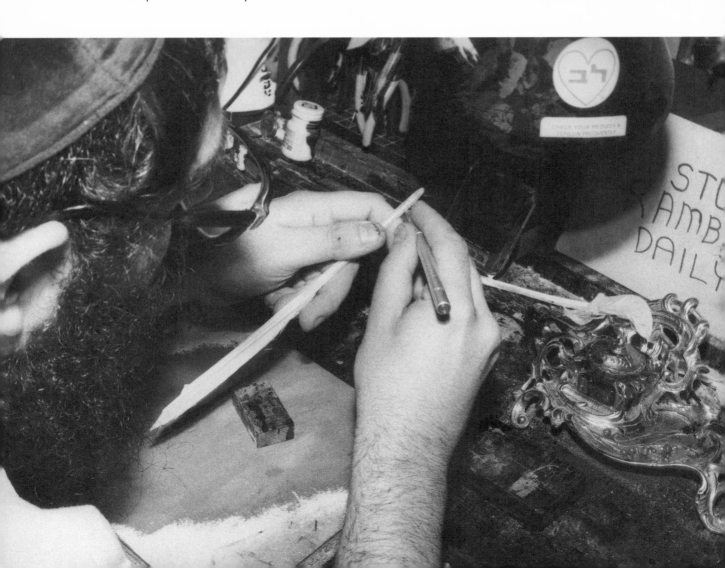

Now that Rabbi Clapman has made the parchment, he must make the ink. He blends gall nuts, copper sulfate crystals, gum arabic, and water; he wants the ink to be strikingly black. To be sure the ink is fresh, he makes only two teaspoonfuls at a time.

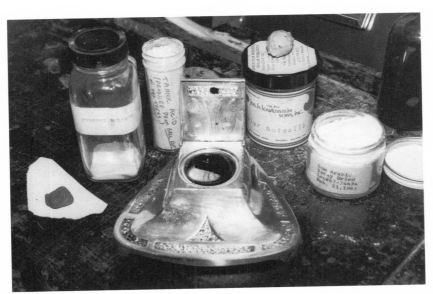

Without quills, the ink is useless. The shape of the quill is very important.

Most quills are made from the outermost five feathers of a kosher bird, such as a goose or a turkey.

Rabbi Clapman likes to use goose feathers because of tradition and because they are large and soft enough to help him write flowing letters. He always buys a large supply of them around Ḥanukkah, the only season of the year they can be acquired in New York.

A scribe writes with the stem of the quill, not the barbs. As a final preparation Rabbi Clapman uses a double-edged razor or a scalpel to put a fine point on the pen.

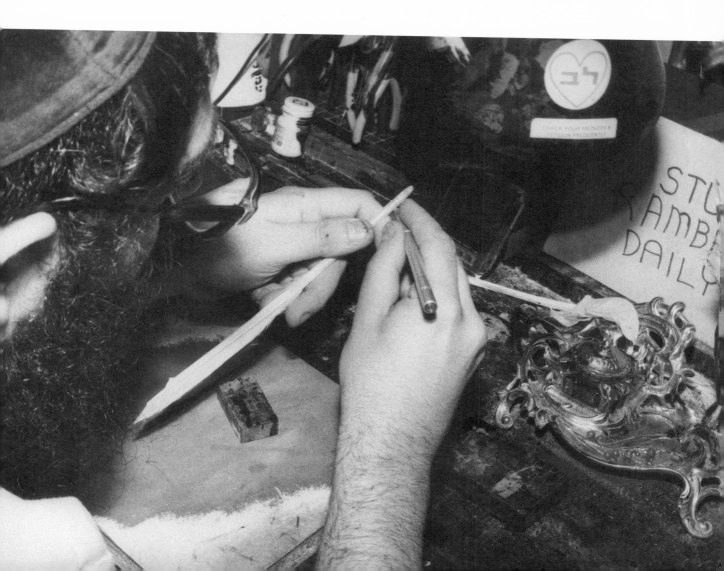

Even the best quill must be sharpened after half a column of writing. That can consume time and feathers. Nevertheless, very skilled scribes, like Rabbi Eliezer Zirkind, develop deft ways of making and using the quills. They need only two or three feathers to write an entire scroll.

It is difficult to make the tip of the quill sharp. Sometimes a scribe can whittle at feathers for a day or two before he has an adequate quill.

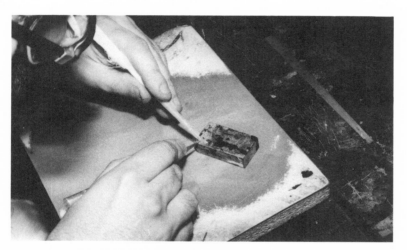

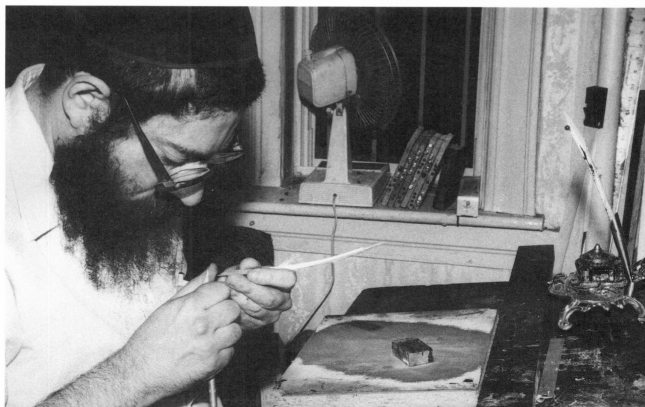

Once the parchment, the ink, and the quill are ready, the *sofer* has all the materials he needs to write.

But he must be sure that his spirit is as prepared as his materials. Before he begins his work each day, he goes to the *mikveh*—the ritual bath—to purify himself. Before he sits down to write he says a special prayer.

The *sofer* is not writing the *sefer Torah* to prove his skill as a craftsman or to earn wages. He seeks to become a human vessel for Divine words. So he prays that the work he performs with his hands will be filled with the holiness he feels in his mind and his heart. He is reminded of that holiness throughout the day, for he must say another special prayer before he writes the Almighty's name.

When a scribe returns from the *mikveh*, he tests his quill and ink before he begins to write. Many scribes make that test by writing the name *Amalek*. Amalekites were an enemy of the Jews; their wickedness was so severe that the Almighty commanded His people to "blot out the memory of Amalek from under heaven."

In keeping with that commandment, which is written in the book of Deuteronomy, scribes blot out the name of Amalek as soon as they write it.

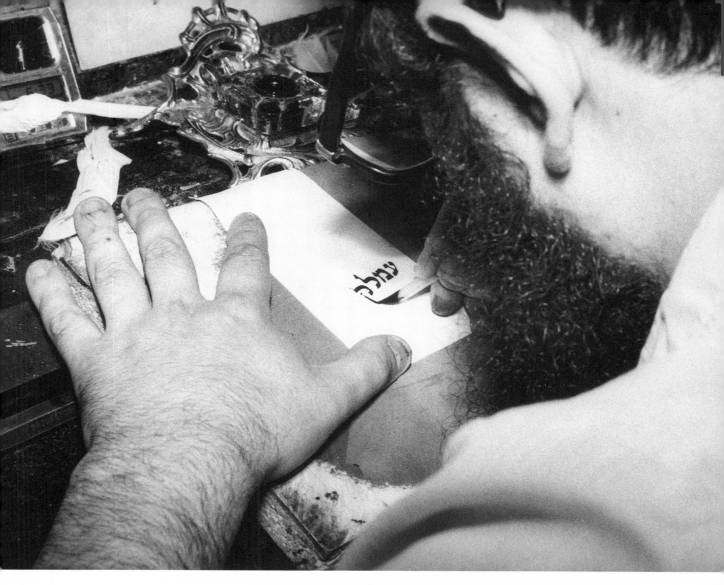

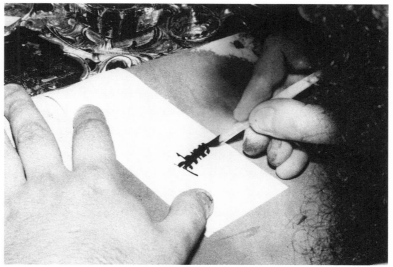

Scribes work under intense pressure, for the completed Torah must be flawless.

Most mistakes can be corrected. The ink can be erased with a knife and a pumice stone.

But a mistake in writing any of the names of the Almighty cannot be corrected. For, according to Jewish law, the Lord's name cannot be erased. When such mistakes are made, the faulty pieces of parchment must be buried.

Thus, for religious reasons and practical ones, scribes do everything in their power to prevent errors.

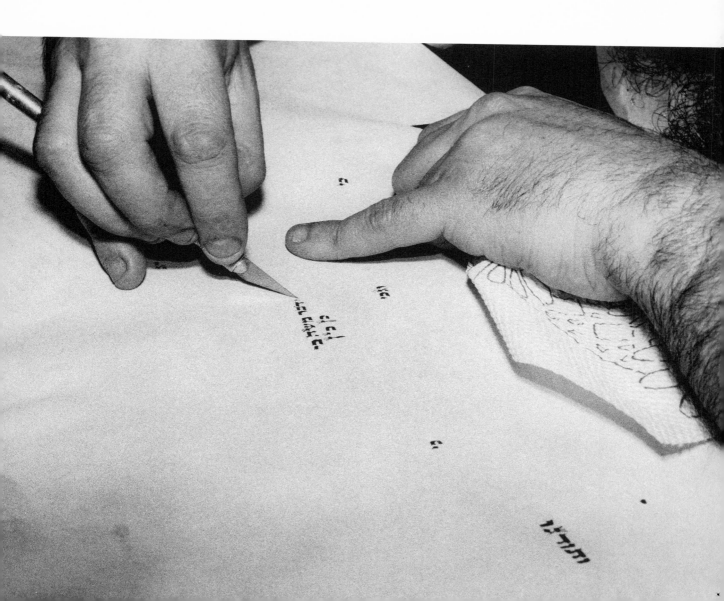

Before a *sofer* writes a word on parchment, he reads it from a specially edited text of the Torah; then he checks it against a printed edition of the Torah to be as sure as possible that there are no mistakes.

It is essential that scribes concentrate. They are not supposed to talk during the hours of the day they are writing the Torah, for conversations distract the mind. If a distraction occurs, the scribe's holy work—and the community's holy life—might suffer.

A scribe's work is extremely demanding. Rabbi Clapman is able to work for about four hours at a time. According to Jewish law, when he is ready to stop, he must make sure he ends each day's labor on a joyous sentence.

If he finishes at night, he doesn't go to sleep until the ink dries. He must be careful about the way he leaves the parchment.

He doesn't want it to remain uncovered overnight. That is disrespectful to the words of the Almighty. On a more practical level, he is worried that particles of dust might get into the ink.

But he doesn't want to preserve the letters by turning the parchment over. If the Almighty's words face downward, that, too, is disrespectful.

He covers the parchment with a piece of wood, making sure that the wood doesn't touch the letters. He places a cloth above it to form a protective covering. That way, its sanctity and purity will be guarded until dawn.

Most scribes take a year to write a *sefer Torah,* although Rabbi Zirkind once finished one in three months.

But no *sofer* is perfect. No matter how carefully he checks his own work, there is still a chance that one of the 248 columns on the sixty to eighty pieces of parchment contains a mistake. So, once the final letter is completed, the painstaking process of inspecting the entire work begins.

If the *sofer* does it alone, he might overlook his own errors. So he teams up with another learned Jew and reads the entire work aloud, letter by letter, line by line, from the first sentence until the last. Often Rabbi Clapman does this with his father. The men repeat that procedure three times. Only then is the text considered fit to be used.

Until the checking is completed, the sixty to eighty pieces of parchment remain in a stack. Then the *sofer* sews the pieces into a scroll.

For this work, he uses *giddin,* a special thread made from the leg sinews of a kosher animal—an ox or a cow or a sheep. (Most scribes prefer to use an ox.) Then the *sofer* threads the *giddin* through needles. He places the sheets of parchment next to each other and uses the *giddin* to sew them together. He makes a stitch on every sixth line.

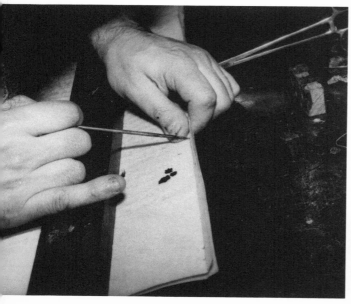

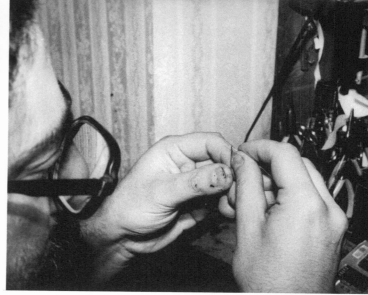

Then he threads the top and the bottom of the parchment together. When that job is finished, the individual sheets become the scroll that will be used in synagogue. Then, each side of the scroll must be sewn onto a wooden handle—the *etz ḥayyim*—before the Torah is ready to be dedicated in a community.

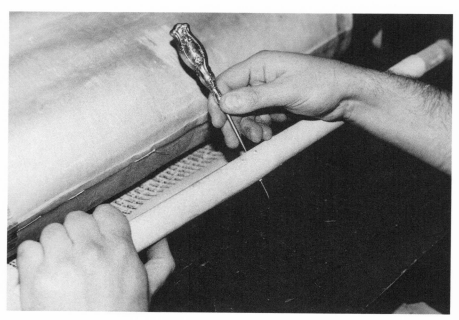

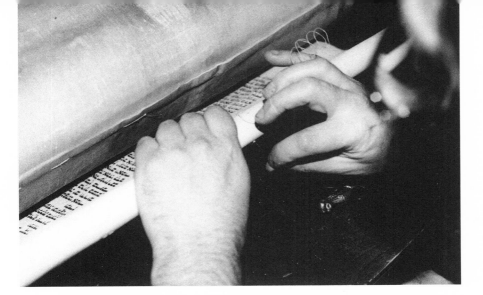

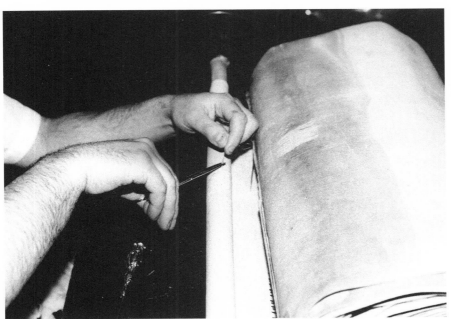

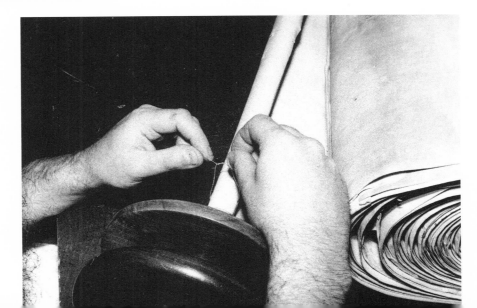

When a new *sefer Torah* is dedicated in a community, the ceremony is almost as joyous as a wedding. Men and women follow, dancing, as the scroll is carried to the synagogue under a canopy. There is dancing with the Torah, and around it, in an exuberant celebration that resembles Simḥat Torah, the day of the Rejoicing of the Law.

No *sefer Torah* is complete until the community participates in finishing it. For, according to Jewish law, a person who completes even one letter of the Torah is regarded as if he has written the entire scroll. And a person who writes a Torah "is regarded as if it had been given to him at Sinai."

Photo by Beryl Goldberg

So scribes like Rabbi Clapman leave the first and last lines of the scrolls they write in outline form. That way, everyone who is present at the joyous ceremony wedding the Torah to the community can fill in a letter. Then, it will be as if all those gathered had been present at Mount Sinai.

Sitting in Rabbi Clapman's work room in Crown Heights, watching him draw lines or mix ink or write letters as his children play merrily outside, you see him as part of a human chain of scribes that stretches through the ages.

These men write the words that bind one generation to the next. They are creating the sacred scroll that Jews have always regarded as "the tree of life . . . whose ways are ways of pleasantness and whose paths are paths of peace."